PRESENTED TO

FROM

DATE

THE GOSPEL IN COLOR - FOR KIDS

Text copyright © 2018 by Curtis A. Woods and Jarvis J. Williams
Illustration copyright © 2018 by Rommel Ruiz

First Edition 2018
Printed in Korea

ISBN-10: 0-9990835-8-9
ISBN-13: 978-0-9990835-8-1
ISBN-10: 0-9990835-9-7 (eBook)
ISBN-13: 978-0-9990835-9-8 (eBook)
Library of Congress Control Number: 2018943144

A **Patrol** Original Book

THE GOSPEL IN COLOR

EDITORIAL

CONTENT DIRECTOR
Eleazar Ruiz

WRITERS
Curtis A. Woods
Jarvis J. Williams

EDITOR
Pip Craighead

CREATIVE

ART DIRECTOR & ILLUSTRATOR
Rommel Ruiz

HEAD OF DESIGN
Eleazar Ruiz

Patrol is a team of storytellers and artists producing books which tell fiction and non-fiction stories inspired by the Bible.

Jesus used storytelling to help people understand spiritual truths about the kingdom of God and its relation to our lives. Following his lead, we use imaginative stories and visuals to communicate biblical truths to all people, including everyday Christians.

Start reading along today!

WeArePatrol.com
@WeArePatrol

CONTENTS

06   **Parents' Guide**
How to Use This Book

08   **Kids' Guide**
How to Use This Book

10   **Introduction**
What's This Book For, Anyway?

16   **Chapter 1**
What Is Race?

30   **Chapter 2**
What Is Racism?

44   **Chapter 3**
What Is the Good News of Jesus Christ?

56   **Chapter 4**
What Is Reconciliation?

72   **Conclusion**
The Gospel in Color

77   **Answer Key**

HOW TO USE THIS BOOK

This book is specifically designed so that your child can dig deep into what the Bible says about race, racism, and reconciliation. These are complex topics, which is why each chapter's content is presented in a way that can engage children at different age levels. To facilitate times of reflection and response, every chapter ends with activities for further study, thought, and prayer.

FOR CHILDREN AGES SIX TO NINE

We recommend reading each chapter with your child, pausing to point out the **Words to Know** definitions and enjoy the illustrations. The imagery and stories throughout the book are there to help your child grasp theological and historical concepts, giving concrete ways to explain creation, the fall, sin, the gospel, redemption, racism, and reconciliation.

After reading and talking about each chapter with your child, go through the **Read & Respond** section, reading the suggested Bible passage and then asking your child the accompanying questions. You can find the answers at the back of the book, and can use these to help coach your child into fully understanding the concepts therein. We suggest reviewing these chapters multiple times, reinforcing the concepts with each reading.

Kids of all ages can **Memorize Scripture**; we encourage you to write down the memory passage from each chapter and place it somewhere you and your child will see it often. Test your child frequently to help them absorb the passage until they know it well. Lastly, the **Ways to Pray** section is designed to help you spend time praying with your child based on the topics of each chapter, utilizing suggested prayer points as well as whatever prayer is on your heart based on the reading.

FOR UPPER ELEMENTARY STUDENTS (AGES TEN AND UP)

This book is also written so that older children can read the book independently. We'd recommend giving your child a journal to use when going through the book. Encourage them to jot down their thoughts and reactions to each chapter, answer questions, write the memory Scripture, and journal their prayers.

After your child has gone through each chapter, start conversations with them about the topics that chapter covered. Ask if there were statements they found challenging or surprising, and seek to explain theological and historical concepts to them as needed. The activity sections are there to help draw connections between theological concepts and children's everyday lives, so we encourage you to ask questions based on those frameworks. Additionally, ask if your child can think of Bible stories and Scripture passages that connect with the themes of each chapter, and make connections to what your church is currently learning on Sundays. Prayer is a vital part of the process, so take time to pray with your child based on what they're learning and how these topics are touching their heart.

KIDS' GUIDE
HOW TO USE THIS BOOK

This book is designed so that kids — like you — can dig deep into what the Bible says about race, racism, and reconciliation. To help you better understand the topics we'll be exploring, each chapter ends with activities for you to complete. This book is also made so that a parent can go through their own version of the book, *The Gospel in Color — For Parents*. Each chapter in that book covers the same themes and highlights the same vocab words, so that you can talk with your parent, ask questions, and pray as you learn together.

Below are the activity sections to keep an eye out for:
- **Read & Respond**: Answer questions based on the Scripture reading for each chapter.
- **Memorize Scripture**: Write down a Scripture relevant to the chapter's theme and commit it to memory.

- **Ways to Pray**: Spend time praying based on the topics of each chapter, utilizing suggested prayer points as well as whatever prayer is on your heart based on the reading.

Our hope is not only that you have fun completing these activities, but that above all, you connect with Jesus through them. God tells us that he is always with us, and so we can talk to him at any point, whether we have questions or simply want to thank him for his goodness. He loves us and promises to hear us when we're seeking him. And that is a wonderful truth indeed.

INTRODUCTION

WHAT'S THIS BOOK FOR, ANYWAY?

BY CURTIS A. WOODS & JARVIS J. WILLIAMS

Racism is real, and it is a sin. All sin is ultimately a spiritual problem, which means it can only find complete healing through Jesus. This book will help you have honest conversations about race, ethnic differences, and racial reconciliation — because Jesus came to heal all our brokenness, including that of racism.

H ave you ever wondered why groups of people look different from one another? Beyond just the differences in the ways people dress or do their hairstyles, people from all over the world look different. Just like a box of crayons, human beings come in a wide variety of colors. But no matter what color our skin is, it's not an accident. It's actually part of God's good design.

As we'll learn together in this book, the Bible tells us that God made human beings "in his image" — meaning they reflect the nature of God. That's something that's true of all people, no matter where they come from or what they look like. God doesn't want us all to look and act exactly the same. The fact that we are all different is actually very beautiful, particularly when we come together to worship Jesus as one big family, just as we see in the book of *Revelation* at the very end of the Bible.

Just like a talent show, all groups of people and all cultures have something special to share with the world. God made us so that in our differences, we would all be unified in our love for Christ.

THE UGLY IDEA

But an idea you have probably heard of — racism — tries to turn God's design upside down. Instead of agreeing with the Bible that all people are made in God's image and are equally valuable, racism says that some people are more valuable than others. This is a complete lie. And like all lies, it causes great pain.

People who believe the lie of racism can do terrible things, whether they're saying something cruel about someone who is different from them or actually attacking them physically. People have killed other people for racist reasons, yet sometimes racism is far more subtle and sneaky — so sneaky it seems almost invisible at first. Racism can be present in words and actions that seem polite, but are actually subtle ways of letting people know they're less valuable because they're different.

In this book, we'll learn about where the lie of racism comes from — and how Jesus wants us to fight this lie.

RACISM SAYS THAT SOME PEOPLE ARE MORE VALUABLE
THAN OTHERS. THIS IS A COMPLETE LIE.
AND LIKE ALL LIES, IT CAUSES GREAT PAIN.

PRETENDING NOT TO SEE

Have you ever heard the word *color-blind*? Being color-blind is a medical condition some people have in which they can't see certain colors. But color-blind is a term with two meanings. Besides describing a medical condition, it can also be used to describe an idea about race some people have. They think that to fight the evil of racism, we should all just pretend not to see the fact that people have different skin colors. They say that we shouldn't acknowledge the fact that we're different, and should just treat everyone the same.

WORD TO KNOW

COLOR-BLINDNESS
The idea that we should ignore people's ethnic differences.

While it's definitely good to treat all people with kindness and respect, that doesn't mean we should pretend that everyone's skin colors are all the same. People around the world have all sorts of different skin colors — and that's not a bad thing. In fact, it's part of God's design!

Instead of pretending that people don't have different skin colors or that racism doesn't exist, we need to discuss these things. Color-blindness won't make racism go away, which is why we need to talk about where racism comes from and how it hurts people. And that's why this book exists.

WHAT THIS BOOK IS ALL ABOUT

This book was written to help you understand different skin colors, ethnic differences, and the evil of racism from a Christian perspective.

The Bible not only shows us where racism ultimately comes from, it tells us how to fight it, and it shows us why all people have dignity and value. Jesus gives us the power to end racism, and the Bible shows us how Jesus' followers accepted and loved each other, no matter how differently they looked or acted.

Each chapter in this book discusses important concepts, and features vivid illustrations to help show the ideas we're talking about. The end of every chapter contains activities, as well as ways to pray so that after reading, you can spend some time talking to Jesus about what you're learning. This book is also designed so that you can learn along with a parent or friend, so that both of you can grow in understanding the Bible and one another.

We're excited to go on this journey with you, and hope you are too! God's word — the Bible — is filled with truth that can change the world and bring healing to our hearts, and Jesus wants to help us understand the power of his love and how it applies to issues of race.

CHAPTER 1

WHAT IS RACE?

BY CURTIS A. WOODS

The beginning of the Bible tells us how God made the world. God created everything good, and all people were made in his image, which means that all people have equal value and worth. Yet some people believe a lie about race that says that some types of people are better than others. Instead of believing this lie, God wants us to honor every skin color.

BEGINNINGS ARE IMPORTANT

Have you ever watched part of a movie, but missed the beginning? Often it can be a confusing experience, as you try to figure out who is who and where the story is going. That's why beginnings are so important — they help us understand what is happening and what to expect in the future.

In our lives today, many people are deeply confused because, just like someone missing the start of a movie, they don't know the beginning of the story of the world. That's one of the reasons God graciously gave us the Bible, which tells us all we need to know about how things began. So when we have questions about skin color, racism, and human relationships, we first look to the Bible, because the Bible shows us the true story of the world. Having a biblical view is key.

THE BEGINNING OF ALL BEGINNINGS

The Bible is made up of different books, and the very first book is called *Genesis* — which literally means "beginning." The beginning of *Genesis* tells us how God created the world out of nothing by speaking light into existence. He made the heavens and the earth. On the earth, he gathered the waters together into the sea and made the dry land appear. God decorated the earth with vegetation that could reproduce all kinds of seeds, fruit, and trees. God made all these things good.

God made the sun and moon, and then he made the land animals and sea creatures — living things which were different but all wonderful. All these creatures were fruitful and multiplied their species on the earth and in the sea. God was pleased with what he had made.

Lastly, God created his crowning jewel — Adam and Eve — in his image, placing them in the Garden of Eden. God made this man and woman so that they would reproduce other stewards over his creation and carry out God's creation mandate together. No other creature could help them fulfill God's command. God was so excited about his creation that he rested to enjoy his artistry.

The story of creation presents a beautiful picture of love. God cared for his creation by crafting a world that could sustain the physical and emotional needs of humanity. The man and woman loved and trusted one another without fear. The animals and sea creatures enjoyed their habitats without territorial fighting. It was literally *all good!*

THE TRUTH ABOUT RACE

The Bible clearly tells us that God created every family from the loving relationship of the first family, Adam and Eve. According to Scripture, every human comes from this same family *(Acts 17:26)*. Every person on earth is made in God's image, and as such, has a unique worth and identity. And all people are **equal** because they are all made in the image of God.

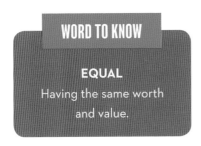

WORD TO KNOW

EQUAL

Having the same worth and value.

Every skin color on the earth points back to the first person created from the earth — Adam. Therefore, God's vision is for all colors to love one another truly, as equals. The Bible rejects the idea of a special race of people who sit above other skin colors.

THE LIE ABOUT RACE

But over time, some people began believing a lie about people who looked different than they did. They said that there are different types of humans, and that some humans are better than others. This imaginary concept of **race** was developed to separate humans based on color. Unlike God's intention to have beautiful variety within his creation, this idea of race lifts up one skin color on the backs of other colors. These racial categories make some people feel better than others, giving them a sense of superiority.

As an example, many Europeans in the 18th century believed they were special above all other cultures. False teachers of the time taught others to see people with dark or brown skin color as inferior beings — despite the fact that they all had the same color of blood running through their veins.

Not only is this very sad, it goes against what God intended. The Bible shows us that there is ultimately only one race: the human race. True love for other colors will never label different hues inferior, and relationships suffer when some people think they are better than other people.

RACE
A word which can simply refer to the human race or a specific ethnic group, but which can be falsely used to mean a category of people with an inherently different value than other people.

EVERY COLOR WAS MADE TO BE LOVED AND CHERISHED,
BECAUSE GOD CREATED ALL THINGS GOOD.

NEW EYES

God wants to give us new eyes to see all the colors of humanity without fear or anger. Every color was made to be loved and cherished, because God created all things good.

You are a part of God's original good creation. He created you the way you are. All human colors are special since they bear God's image.

So where does the destructive lie of racism actually come from? What is its ultimate root? The beginning of the Bible contains the answer to those questions, as we'll see in the next chapter!

READ & RESPOND

Read the creation account in *Genesis 1-2* and answer the following questions.

1 In *Genesis 1:31*, what did God say when he surveyed everything that he had made?

2 What does *Genesis 1:26-27* tell us about all human beings? In whose image are they made?

3 What does this tell us about the value of people of different skin colors?

4 How do you think God wants you to treat other people made in the image of God through your thoughts, speech, and actions regardless of whether those people share your skin color?

MEMORIZE SCRIPTURE

Write down the following Scripture and commit it to memory: Psalm 139:14.

WAYS TO PRAY

Below are prayer points to help you talk to God about what you're learning. We encourage you to speak to him in your own words, knowing he is always ready to hear his children.

Give God thanks for the fact that he made the world and all things in it, and praise him that you have the honor of being made in the image of God.

Give God praise that the way he made you — including your skin color and ethnic background — is no mistake, and that your skin color and ethnic heritage are good.

Pray that God would give you eyes to see his hand in the wonderful diversity of all people in the world, and thank him that he is the God of every tribe, tongue, people, and nation.

Write your own prayer to God, in your own words, based on the topics covered in this chapter.

CHAPTER 2

WHAT IS RACISM?

BY CURTIS A. WOODS

BIG IDEA

The Bible tells us that God created our world good, but when people rebelled against God, sin appeared. Sin brought evil and sadness into our world, and is the reason people hurt and hate one another. The lie of racism has led to great pain and evil, and still hurts people today. That's why it's so important that we look to Jesus and speak truth.

THE BIG LIE

As we saw in the last chapter, God made the world very good. Adam and Eve dwelled in a beautiful garden, living in harmony with God and each other. But one day, something terrible happened — something which led to all the other sad things in the world today, including racism.

Genesis 3 tells us a serpent lied to Eve, saying that God wanted to withhold something good from the first family. Eve listened to the serpent and the desires of her own heart, questioning God's goodness.

WORD TO KNOW

SIN
An act of rebellion against God and his good laws.

Eve doubted God's word, and decided to do things her way instead of God's. She wanted to act like her own god by obeying her own sinful desires.

Both Adam and Eve chose to believe the big lie: that God could not be trusted.

When Adam and Eve believed this lie and disobeyed God, **sin** entered humanity. Sin is rebellion against God and his commands, and it is the cause of everything sad and wrong in our world.

WORD TO KNOW

RACISM

The poisonous idea of people or governments rewarding social and economic privileges to one group of people by virtue of skin color or ethnic background.

Adam and Eve's sin led to global strife on earth. Men and women had fights with one another. The process of farming and getting food became burdensome. Animals attacked humans and ate other animals. God had created a peaceful, beautiful world, but sin birthed chaos. The chaos of sin means that creation experiences disorder, trouble, and confusion.

THE SIN OF RACISM

Because of sin, our world is filled with struggle, and the serpent continues to spread lies about God's original good creation. Over the many centuries since Adam and Eve, people have been deceived by these lies and have shared them with other people. One of these lies is **racism**, which is based on the false concept of race that we talked about in the last chapter.

The lie of racism was widespread through Europe during the 18th century and beyond. Instead of believing that all humans were ultimately one race created by God, people taught the lie that God created multiple races of humans. Many of these thinkers viewed some people as members of different species. In other words, they said that people who were different than them were not fully human. This is a lie from the old serpent, and goes against what the Bible teaches.

Some people even tried to distort what the Bible says to support their racist beliefs. Imagine how God feels when people twist his word to support lies. That's why it is so important to read the Bible the way the Author meant it to be understood, and to avoid reading racist ideas into biblical stories.

RACISM AND SLAVERY

One of the saddest things about the history of racism is how people who had the power to bully others treated certain image-bearers like disposable items. They labeled some colors superior and others inferior. In world history, "lesser" colors were captured, placed in warehouses, and transported all over the globe like cargo in the bottom of rat-filled boats. Children were kidnapped from their mothers and fathers. Whole families were put in chains, then separated and sold — they were

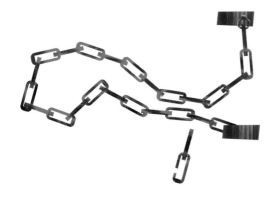

treated just like property. People often died during these voyages to slave ports around the world.

This was something that many Europeans and Americans did to Africans over the centuries, before it was made illegal. Like true bullies, the villains who kidnapped, bought, and sold these victims did not believe enslaved people possessed human dignity. The truth is that anytime we treat humans like disposable items it delights the devil, but dishonors God.

RACISM CAUSES GREAT PAIN

Racism — even when it doesn't involve slavery — is still around today. Racism often happens when a society passes laws that make it hard for certain people to succeed. Racism takes place when certain skin colors are labeled problems even before problems occur. Racism can happen in sneaky ways as well as obvious ones. Racism occurs when people don't get a job just because they have a certain skin color or look different.

ALL CHRISTIANS ARE CALLED TO HONOR GOD
BY SPEAKING THE TRUTH AGAINST RACISM
IN A GRACIOUS WAY.

Have you ever played a game like "cooties," where you pretend that somebody has an imaginary disease, and that you can't touch them? The game can become mean, as children laugh and point at some innocent child falsely declared "cooties." That child can end up feeling shamed, hurt, and alone.

That's what racism does in society. It hurts and shames people who have been labeled "problems." Racism is profoundly evil.

WHERE DO WE GO FROM HERE?

All Christians are called to honor God by speaking the truth against racism in a gracious way. That means you no longer see people who have racist ideas as the enemy. They are victims of your enemy. When you encounter a person who hates people because of their skin color, you are hearing the serpent's voice.

But there's good news — incredibly good news, as a matter of fact. Racism will not be victorious in our world, because Jesus came to heal the impact that Adam and Eve's sin brought upon the entire world. In the next chapter, we'll talk about how Jesus restores our relationship with God and each other, and brings victory over racism and every other sin.

WHAT IS RACISM?

READ & RESPOND

Read the account of the fall of humanity in *Genesis 3* and answer the following questions.

1 According to *Genesis 3:1-6*, how does sin start? What kind of attitude did Adam and Eve have toward God?

2 What were the consequences of Adam and Eve's sin?

3 How does the sin of racism directly go against what God says in the Bible?

4 How does racism hurt people today?

MEMORIZE SCRIPTURE

Write down the following Scripture and commit it to memory: *Romans 6:23.*

WAYS TO PRAY

Below are prayer points to help you talk to God about what you're learning. We encourage you to speak to him in your own words, knowing he is always ready to hear his children.

Pray that Jesus would help you see all people as worthy of dignity and respect because they are made in the image of God.

Have you ever been cruel to someone because they were different, whether they had a different skin color or simply acted differently than you? If so, ask God for forgiveness for that sin, and ask him to give you wisdom in how to apologize to that person, if at all possible.

Is there anybody you have a hard time showing kindness to because they are different than you? Ask the Lord to help you see that person the way he would have you see them — as someone loved by God.

Is there anybody in your life who you have heard say something racist? If so, pray for that person, and ask God for wisdom on any ways you can lovingly, graciously correct those words (check in with your parent for advice on this). Ask God to heal any pain those racist words have caused you.

Write your own prayer to God, in your own words, based on the topics covered in this chapter.

CHAPTER 3

WHAT IS THE GOOD NEWS OF JESUS CHRIST?

BY JARVIS J. WILLIAMS

BIG IDEA

The gospel is the good news that Jesus came to undo the curse of sin that came as a result of Adam and Eve's rebellion. Instead of giving up on his people, God sent his Son to live a perfect life, die on the cross, and rise again, forgiving us of our sins — including the sin of racism. Jesus brings healing to all the world's divisions.

VERY, VERY, VERY GOOD NEWS

You know the feeling of sharing good news with a friend? Maybe the good news is that you made a new friend, or that someone you know who was sick is now feeling better. Whatever the news, it is exciting to share something happy with someone else.

Well, the Bible contains something very special: it contains the best news that anyone has ever heard! In fact, you could call it very, very, very good news — the best news of all. But to really understand this good news, we have to look at the whole story of the Bible.

Ready? Let's go!

THE PROBLEM OF SIN

As we saw in Chapter 1, the Bible starts with God making the whole world — the planets, sun, and stars, as well as our earth and everything in it. He made the animals and then, last of all, he made the first people, Adam and Eve. Adam and Eve lived in a beautiful garden, and were friends with God. Being friends with God is a wonderful thing — it's actually the most wonderful thing there is.

But after Adam and Eve believed the lie and disobeyed God, their relationship with God and with each other was broken. When they rebelled against God, sin came into the world — and when sin came, it ruined everything.

Because of sin, people aren't friends with God anymore.

Because of sin, people and the rest of creation experience death.

Because of sin, people fight with each other and say hurtful things to one another.

Because of sin, people don't like each other because of how they look or what color their skin is.

Sin is the reason there is so much sadness in the world, and it is the big problem beneath every other problem. Every war, every death, every sad thing is because of sin.

WHAT IS THE GOOD NEWS OF JESUS CHRIST?

GOD LOVES PEOPLE TOO MUCH TO LET THE STORY END
WITH ADAM AND EVE'S SIN.

HOPE FOR THE WORLD

God loves people too much to let the story end with Adam and Eve's sin. In fact, he promised his people that one day, there would come a Savior to rescue the world from sin and death.

Many centuries passed, and during that time, sin led to more and more trouble, pain, and evil. One of those evils is called *division*, which is what happens when people refuse to be friends with people who are somehow different than them. Racism, which we talked about in the previous chapter, is a form of sinful division.

But about 2,000 years ago, to everyone's surprise, God himself came into the story of our world to rescue it! Jesus Christ was born a Jewish man, but while he was fully a human being, he was also God. It's hard to completely understand how such a thing could be, but nothing is impossible for God.

HOW JESUS BRINGS HEALING

Jesus lived a perfect life, healing people, showing love to people, and sharing the news of God's kingdom. Jesus invited people into God's kingdom, telling them that God cared about them and wanted them to act in love and kindness with one another the way that Jesus acted in love and kindness.

Jesus showed his love in the most powerful way possible: by dying for our sins. See, each of us has sinned in our lives one way or another, and since sin is an act of rebellion against God, it deserves punishment. In addition to our personal sins, the presence of sin has messed up the whole world. But since God wants to forgive us, he actually took the punishment for our sin himself when Jesus died upon the cross.

WORD TO KNOW

RESURRECTION

The act of someone being raised from death to life. Jesus was resurrected after his death on the cross, and because of Jesus, all who believe in his name have the future promise of being raised from death to everlasting life.

After Jesus died, he was buried in a rock tomb. But three days later, he rose again — he was no longer dead, but alive forevermore. The **resurrection** of Jesus shows that God is stronger than death. After his resurrection, Jesus told his followers to go and tell the whole world about him.

Because Jesus is alive, the whole world can experience forgiveness and healing.

Because Jesus is alive, death will ultimately be done away with.

Because Jesus is alive, people can be friends with God forever!

That's the very, very, very good news we talked about at the beginning of this chapter. The **gospel** is the good news of Jesus' life, death, and resurrection, which brings the kingdom of God to our world. The gospel results in the forgiveness of sin — including the sin of racism. That means that followers of Jesus should no longer be divided because of how they look or what color their skin is.

This is good news for our world! In the next chapter, we'll talk about how the gospel powerfully brings about reconciliation to people divided by racism.

READ & RESPOND

Read 1 Corinthians 15:20-23 and answer the following questions.

1 Who is the man who brought death in *1 Corinthians 15:21*, and who is the man who brought the resurrection of the dead?

2 How does Jesus' death pay the price for all our sins? What does that mean for your life and your sins?

3 How is Jesus' life, death, and resurrection the greatest reason for rejoicing that we could ever hear? How does it bring healing to the world, including people of every skin color?

4 What do you think it means to "belong to Christ" as mentioned in *1 Corinthians 15:23*? How can you live as somebody who belongs to Christ, including through the way you treat people of different skin colors and backgrounds?

MEMORIZE SCRIPTURE

Write down the following Scripture and commit it to memory: *John 1:29*.

WAYS TO PRAY

Below are prayer points to help you talk to God about what you're learning. We encourage you to speak to him in your own words, knowing he is always ready to hear his children.

Thank God for the forgiveness and redemption we have in Jesus' freely given sacrifice. Rejoice in the fact that the Lord counts you as a beloved son or daughter because you've put your faith in him.

Pray that everyone in your family would continually turn to Jesus for forgiveness and restoration whenever they sin, knowing that Christ has already paid the price for sinners — including if they sin by regarding one skin color as better than another.

Pray that people all over the world who do not know Jesus would come to experience forgiveness and peace with God through the gospel. Pray that this good news would bring healing to all those who are divided over skin color and other issues.

Is there anyone you know who you'd like to share the good news of Jesus with? Ask God how you can tell them about Jesus, and pray for an opportunity to share this exciting news with them. Ask your parent for advice on how to share the gospel.

Write your own prayer to God, in your own words, based on the topics covered in this chapter.

CHAPTER 4

WHAT IS RECONCILIATION

BY JARVIS J. WILLIAMS

BIG IDEA

Jesus came to bring peace between all sorts of people — no matter how different they may seem. This reconciliation is one of the results of the gospel, and brings healing to the divisions caused by racism. In Jesus, God calls his people to love and forgive one another, regardless of our countries, cultures, or colors.

THE SON WHO RAN AWAY

Have you ever been cruel to someone, or had someone be cruel to you? It can cause great pain and sadness to everyone involved. But when someone says sorry, that is the start of **reconciliation** – when two people who were separated as enemies come together as friends.

During his ministry on earth, Jesus told his followers a powerful story about reconciliation. It's known as the story of the Prodigal Son.

GOD IS A LOVING FATHER
WHO WANTS TO WELCOME US HOME.

WHAT IS RECONCILIATION?

RECONCILIATION

The restoration of a previously broken relationship between people.

A father had two sons. The older son worked hard for his father, but one day, the younger son asked his father to give him money so that he could do what he wanted with it. The father gave his son what he asked for. The younger son left his family to go away to a far country, where he wasted all of his money on partying and selfish things.

After wasting his money, the younger son was hungry, so hungry that he even wished he could eat what pigs eat. So he went back home to beg for his father's forgiveness and ask if he could work hard for his father in exchange for food. Do you think the father would be happy to see his younger son, or angry with how selfishly his son had left the family and wasted all his money?

Well, when the father saw his younger son coming from a distance, he rushed to meet him. He embraced him and kissed him. He was so thankful to have his son home.

The father celebrated his son's return with a party. The older son who had stayed home and served his father complained that his father had showed his younger son too much affection. The father told his older son that the son who returned was lost, but now was found. His return home was a reason to celebrate!

GOD RECONCILES US

The father's response to his younger son is a beautiful picture of reconciliation. The younger son acted as an enemy when he abandoned his father. But when he returned to his father after coming to his senses, the father received his son as a friend. This is what reconciliation is all about.

Reconciliation is something we all need. That's actually what the good news of Jesus is all about — God came to reconcile us even though we had sinned against him and treated him as an enemy. Jesus came to heal us, forgive us, and bring us back into full friendship with our Creator and other people. Jesus came to reconcile the entire world, the entire universe, to himself!

God is a loving Father who wants to welcome us home.

GOD BRINGS US TOGETHER

Reconciliation is not only something that happens between us and God. It's also something that God brings about between ourselves and other people — including people divided over race. Reconciliation is not optional!

As we've seen in previous chapters, the sin of racism makes people enemies of one another based on their skin colors or where they come from. But Jesus came to reconcile enemies and make them friends. Jesus died on the cross for all our sins — including the sin of racism. As a result, people who believe in Jesus are brothers and sisters in Christ, no matter what we look like.

In fact, Jesus brings together all sorts of different people — from every tribe and people and language all over the world — and makes them one big family: the family of God. Because they are God's family, all followers of Jesus are to peacefully live with one another despite their differences — in **unity**. For Christians, we must absolutely oppose racism, because it is an attack upon our unity as brothers and sisters in Christ.

WORD TO KNOW

UNITY
When people are peacefully joined together in love even when there is disagreement.

FORGIVING THOSE WHO SIN AGAINST US

Jesus calls us to love our neighbor as ourselves — which means we should treat people in a way that shows them they are loved and valued, because Jesus loves and values them. Loving people also means forgiving them if they do something wrong to us, including if they display racism by their words or actions. Forgiveness can feel very hard sometimes. Jesus knows how hard it can be — he died on the cross in order to forgive us, even though it was the most painful experience possible. But because Jesus died on the cross, he enables us to forgive people for their sins against us.

Forgiving someone doesn't mean we pretend we aren't hurt, and it doesn't mean we just ignore whatever they do. Forgiveness means we don't retaliate with hate, but commit to loving them instead. Even when we forgive someone, the process of reconciliation means they must still seek to make things right, undo damage they've done, and face the consequences of their actions.

We can't do these things on our own — so we must ask Jesus to help us to do them. We can rely on his power and help to forgive others, to seek reconciliation, and to display unity as followers of Jesus. In so doing, we help show people how great and wonderful God is, and that he is stronger than any evil, including racism!

WHAT IS RECONCILIATION?

READ & RESPOND

Read the story of the Prodigal Son from *Luke 15:11-32* and answer the following questions.

1 In *Luke 15:20-24*, how do we see the father in the story seek reconciliation with his son?

2 In *Luke 15:18-21*, what attitude did the son have when seeking reconciliation with his father?

3 What would it look like if the father and son had not reconciled?

4 Why might some people not want to seek reconciliation with people who are different from them?

MEMORIZE SCRIPTURE

Write down the following Scripture and commit it to memory:
Romans 5:10.

WAYS TO PRAY

Below are prayer points to help you talk to God about what you're learning. We encourage you to speak to him in your own words, knowing he is always ready to hear his children.

Pray for people who believe the lie of racism, that the Holy Spirit would open their eyes to the truth that all people are made in God's image.

Pray that God would bring all Christians together in unity as one family in Jesus, and that God would change us and remove all forms of racism from our hearts.

Has anyone in your life made you feel bad because you're different from them? Ask God to help you to forgive them and seek reconciliation with them. Ask your mom or dad for advice on how to respond when this person is cruel.

Is there anyone you know who seems very different from you? Ask God how you can reach out to show the love and kindness of Jesus to them.

Write your own prayer to God, in your own words, based on the topics covered in this chapter.

CONCLUSION

THE GOSPEL IN COLOR

BY CURTIS A. WOODS & JARVIS J. WILLIAMS

SEEING THE STORY IN FULL COLOR

Imagine if some friends told you they have an incredible TV, and invite you over to their house to see it. But when they show you their TV, it only displays black and white pictures, with no color. Your friends would be missing out on a dazzling variety of colors, and not seeing movies and shows as they were made to be seen. A color screen gives a fuller picture, showing the image as it was intended to be.

That's why it's so important that we see God's world as it was meant to be seen — in color! And that's why this book is called *The Gospel in Color*, because we want everyone to see the good news of Jesus in all its glorious fullness and color.

Our hope is that kids, parents, and teachers alike would celebrate the fact that Jesus came to set us free from the sin of racism, and to bring racial reconciliation to all people. This is good news, and the whole world needs to hear it!

FIVE WAYS TO LIVE OUT THE GOSPEL IN COLOR

The gospel isn't something we're supposed to just learn about — it's something that's supposed to affect how we live our daily lives. To help you in that process, below are five ways you can live out the gospel in color. These may not always be easy to do, but if we look to Jesus and rely on the power of his Spirit, he will guide and equip us as we seek to follow him together.

1.   **Become** friends with people who are different than you — whether they come from a different country, have a different skin color, or speak a different language. Just because someone is different doesn't mean you can't be wonderful friends, especially if you are both followers of Jesus.

2.   **Admit** when you may see people with different skin colors as enemies. Instead of being fearful or mean to them, seek to pursue friendship and reconciliation with them.

3.   Always **remember** that you are wonderfully made in the image of God, and that no color is better or worse than another color.

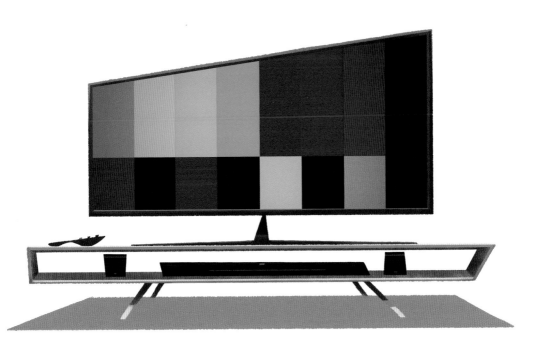

4. **Be honest** when you feel sad, angry, or hurt because of racism. Share your feelings with a parent or trusted friend, and most importantly, talk to God about how this makes you feel. Listen to other people when they express how they are affected by racism as well.

5. **Share** the gospel in color with other people! Tell them how Jesus came to set us free from sin and heal all divisions, including those based on skin color. This good news is something to celebrate every day and tell other people about. Jesus told us to proclaim the gospel to the whole world — which means people of every skin color, language, and nation!

A FINAL ENCOURAGEMENT

We hope you've found this book to be a helpful companion for understanding race, reconciliation, and the life-changing power of the gospel. Our prayer is that you've experienced wonderful times of discussion and prayer when reading this with a parent or friend.

We're honored to have been able to share this book with you, and we thank you for going on this journey with us. Together, let's keep looking to Jesus and continue to pray that he will draw his people closer together, until the day we all celebrate him in the new creation!

ANSWER KEY

CHAPTER 1
WHAT IS RACE?

1. **In *Genesis 1:31*, what did God say when he surveyed everything that he had made?**

   God said that it was very good.

2. **What does *Genesis 1:26-27* tell us about all human beings? In whose image are they made?**

   All people, male and female, are made in the image of God, and have been given dominion over their fellow creatures.

3. **What does this tell us about the value of people of different skin colors?**

   That we are all equally made in the image of God.

4. **How do you think God wants you to treat other people made in the image of God through your thoughts, speech, and actions — regardless of whether those people share your skin color?**

   God wants us to treat all people with dignity, respect, and love in what we think, say, and do.

CHAPTER 2
WHAT IS RACISM?

1. **According to _Genesis 3:1-6_, how does sin start? What kind of attitude did Adam and Eve have toward God?**
   Adam and Eve listened to the serpent rather than God. Instead of trusting the Lord, they doubted that what God said was true and that his way was what was best for them.

2. **What were the consequences of Adam and Eve's sin?**
   Death. Their eyes were opened, they became aware of their nakedness, and they hid from God's presence. They sought to blame others for their choices, and from that point on, experienced pain and struggle in their lives. They were cast out from Eden and would eventually die, returning to the ground from which they were taken.

3. **How does the sin of racism directly go against what God says in the Bible?**
   Racism denies that all people are made in the image of God and shows the kind of partiality that God forbids. Instead of loving our neighbor as ourselves, racism shows love to some and cruelty to others.

4. **How does racism hurt people today?**
   Racism excludes people on an individual and group level.

CHAPTER 3
WHAT IS THE GOOD NEWS OF JESUS CHRIST?

1. **Who is the man who brought death in *1 Corinthians 15:21*, and who is the man who brought the resurrection of the dead?**
    Adam is the man who brought death; Jesus is the man who brought resurrection from the dead.

2. **How does Jesus' death pay the price for all our sins? What does that mean for your life and your sins?**
    Jesus' perfect life fulfilled the law, and he died in our place on the cross, taking our sin upon himself in order to bring about reconciliation between us and God. This atoning death means that when you place your faith in Jesus, you are forgiven and have peace with God.

3. **How is Jesus' life, death, and resurrection the greatest reason for rejoicing that we could ever hear? How does it bring healing to the world, including people of every skin color?**
    Jesus' life, death, and resurrection confront the problem for everything wrong and broken in our world: sin. Jesus came so that everybody everywhere could experience forgiveness for sin and restored fellowship with God and one another, regardless of their skin color and background.

4. **What do you think it means to "belong to Christ" as mentioned in *1 Corinthians 15:23*? How can you live as somebody who belongs to Christ, including through the way you treat people of different skin colors and backgrounds?**

    Answers may vary, but to belong to Christ is to be someone who has placed their faith in Jesus and is committed to following him. As a result, we will show gospel-motivated love to people of all skin colors and backgrounds, seeking to demonstrate and share the good news of Jesus with them.

CHAPTER 4
WHAT IS RECONCILIATION?

1. **In *Luke 15:20-24*, how do we see the father in the story seek reconciliation with his son?**

    He runs to his son and welcomes him back with open arms. The father clothes his son, shows him forgiveness, and throws a party to celebrate his son's return.

2. **In *Luke 15:18-21*, what attitude did the son have when seeking reconciliation with his father?**

    The son acknowledged his sin, said he was no longer worthy of his father's love, and hoped that his father would treat him as a hired servant instead of a son.

3. **What would it look like if the father and son had not reconciled?**

    Children can use their imaginations here, but in any case, the younger son would experience alienation and loneliness, while the father would not experience the joy of reunion with his son. Neither would experience reconciliation.

4. **Why might some people not want to seek reconciliation with people who are different from them?**
    A variety of answers are possible, including fear, hatred, unforgiveness, not understanding the gospel, not wishing to experience fellowship and unity with others who are different from them, etc.

NOTES

NOTES

NOTES